LITERATURE & WRITING WORKSHOP

EXPLORING
LYRIC POETRY

TEACHER'S SOURCEBOOK

SCHOLASTIC INC.

CONTENTS

EDITORIAL—*Editor:* Deborah Jerome-Cohen • *Literature Research:* Eileen Burke, Teresa Cullen • *Sourcebook Writer:* Tara McCarthy

ART—*Art Director:* Patricia Isaza • *Computer Design:* Marjorie Campolongo

EDITORIAL ADMINISTRATION—*Editor-in-Chief:* Terry Cooper

PUBLISHING—*Vice President, Professional Publishing:* Claudia Cohl • *Vice President, Circulation and Marketing:* Stephen Bernard • *Marketing Director:* Jane Fisher • *Marketing Manager:* Melanie Seto • *Fulfillment Manager:* Joan Marcelynas • *Business Manager:* Beth Polcari • *Promotion Design Director:* Dale Moyer • *Promotion Manager:* Carol Skolnick • *Manager, Product Manufacturing:* Laurie Giannelli

ADVISORY BOARD—Karen D'Angelo Bromley, Professor, the School of Education and Human Development, Binghamton University, Binghamton, NY • Eileen Burke, Chairperson, the Reading and Lanugage Department, Trenton State University, Trenton, NJ • Doris Dillon, Primary Language Arts Resource Teacher, San Jose Unified School District, San Jose, CA • Theresa Hancock, 5th grade teacher, Brookside Elementary School, Worthington, OH • Suzanne Houghton, 4th grade teacher, Grace Church School, New York, NY • Lynn Parsons, 5th grade teacher, Stratham Memorial School, Stratham, NH

ART CREDIT—Illustrations on pages 2, 8, 11, 12, 14, 16: Ellen Joy Sasaki. Illustrations on title page, pages 2, 18, 33 and 41: Tony DeLuna. Illustrations on pages 2, 25, 29, 30 37: Chi Chung. Photo on page 6: AP/WideWorld Photos. Photo on page 7: Marion Morehouse.

ISBN 0-590-49305-1

hen a child begins to write a story with "Once upon a time" and tells of magic spells or characters who live happily ever after as a reward for their kindness or heroism, it's clear that the inspiration is coming from the storybooks the child has read or heard. Recent studies on the reading-writing connection have pointed to a simple, important truth: Children who are exposed to literature incorporate ideas and literary structures into the writing of their own stories.

This connection between reading and writing has inspired a unique program: The Scholastic Literature & Writing Workshop provides everything you need to get students excited about literature and to get them to use what they read as models for what they write.

In focusing on the elements of the genre or a kind of writing, and in giving students practice with these elements, you will be making students aware that language and literature have structures—structures that can be understood. The Literature & Writing Workshop helps students deepen their appreciation for literature and writing by giving them high-quality works and the precise tools for building their own narratives.

Developed by teachers for teachers, the Literature & Writing Workshop reflects the latest thinking in promoting literacy: The program is inquiry-based, child-centered, and provides plenty of opportunity for students to make choices and follow their own particular enthusiasms. Many activities in the program are also designed to foster a cooperative sharing of knowledge and ideas.

PROGRAM MANAGEMENT

evoting three to four weeks to Exploring Lyric Poetry will allow students to become truly immersed in poetry formats and their structure. This sourcebook will help students analyze what they read, react to what they learn, and use their new knowledge to create their own lyric poems.

On the next page you will find a chart showing you how the program is organized. For each section in the anthology, you will find teaching strategies for introducing and analyzing the selections, as well as discussion ideas. All the activities in the sourcebook can be done individually or as a group. The three sections are arranged in order of difficulty—from the simple lyricism of "In Quiet Night" to the more intricate, complex poetry of Robert Frost's "Stopping By Woods on a Snowy Evening."

Literature & Writing Workshop

INTRODUCING THE GENRE

- calling on prior knowledge
- defining the genre
- special genre terms

SECTION 1

- background info, teaching tips
- prereading, postreading activities and responses
- exploring a literary device

SECTION 2

- background info, teaching tips
- prereading, postreading activities and responses
- exploring a literary device

SECTION 3

- background info, teaching tips
- prereading, postreading activities and responses
- exploring a literary device

ANALYZING THE THREE SECTIONS

- compare/contrast story elements
- refine the definition of the genre

EXTENDING THE READING

- outside reading in the genre
- cross-curricular activities

WRITING AN ORIGINAL GENRE PIECE

- brainstorming and research
- developing specific elements
- outlining, drafting, conferencing
- revising and publishing

Dear Parent:

The Scholastic Literature & Writing Workshop is a unique program designed to introduce your child to different writing styles and to help your child develop as an analytical, appreciative reader and capable writer.

Exploring Lyric Poetry is part of a 16-unit series that includes such literary forms as biography, humor, and plays. As your child works with this unit, he or she will read many examples of lyric poetry, analyze them, and use what has been learned to write his or her own poetry.

Here are a few ways to enhance your child's study of lyric poetry:

- The rhythms and sounds of poetry are all everywhere. Since your child may most often hear them via lyrics in pop songs on radio, TV, and tape recordings, capitalize on this exposure by listening along and commenting on the rhyming words you hear. Invite your child to tap out with you with the rhythms you discern.

  The fun of poetry is often captured in playground rhymes and game-calls:

  > One potato, two potato,
  > Three potato, *four*,
  > Five potato, six potato,
  > Seven potato *more*?

  Share these old rhymes with your children and invite them to share the new versions with you, noting the rhythms and the rhyming words.

- The beauty of poetry is in its concise word pictures and the images it suggests. Find and read aloud from anthologies or remember and recite from memory the special poems that moved you when you were a child. Explain why you liked these poems and what you imagined while you were hearing them.

- Help your child note that poetry grows out of observations we make and imagery we use to describe things. For example, "that cloud looks like a ship with sails;" or "a frog is a friendly voice in a pond." Make a "Poetry Prize" space on your family bulletin board for posting poetic images your child and other family members come up with.

- Invite your child to read aloud to you poems from this anthology that he or she likes especially. Respond by telling why *you* like the poems, and suggest that you and your child read the poems aloud together.

Happy reading!

About Lyric Poetry

William Shakespeare

The literary term *lyric poetry* goes back in history to the times when poetry was inalterably connected with song; thus its root in the Greek *lura*, "lyre" (the musical instrument which poetic words were designed to accompany). As time went on, poetry developed in ways that began to separate it from a direct dependence on a musical instrument. There came *dramatic poetry,* used in the rhythmic, sonorous lines of Greek plays, Shakespeare's plays and Robert Browning's *Dramatic Monologues.* There came *narrative poetry,* used in ancient ballads as a way of news-reporting, and still used today as a way of telling stories in rhyme. (An example is Longfellow's "Paul Revere.") The term *lyric poetry* lingered as a way of identifying those forms of poetry built around rhythmic, rhyming song-like qualities, such as sonnets, odes, hymns, and elegies, rather than poems designed to tell stories or present dramas.

The other elements of lyric poetry that often distinguish it from narrative and dramatic poetry are its purposeful, aimed-for *subjectivity* and *appeal to the senses.* Today, it is mainly these characteristics that make us classify some poems as *lyric* poems. Today we also have lyric poems with lines set as speech-patterns, or lyric poems that are *free verse,* liberating poets to capture on paper highly idiosyncratic ways of expressing their feelings and telling about images. The lyric poems in the accompanying anthology represent both old and new forms.

An Approach to Teaching Poetry

■ **Organization of the Anthology** In the anthology, the lyric poetry is organized in three sections: nature, people, and thoughts and feelings. This organization was chosen to help ease children into *writing* lyric poetry. It's usually "easiest" to write about the nonhuman world, a little more challenging to write perceptively about people, and often most difficult to write poetry about our personal, inner life. Of course, these categories overlap: It's almost impossible to write a poem about a bird, for example, without revealing how we feel about the bird.

■ **The Recursive Approach** There are basic literary strategies that apply to all lyric poetry. Chief among these are *imagery* and *feeling.* Also important is *form*: Will I set my poem up in a traditional rhythm-and-rhyme lines? break the lines to show natural speech patterns? use free verse to try to capture the ebb and flow of my feelings? Because these strategies are all-encompassing, the sourcebook uses a recursive approach to come back to them all again and again from slightly different angles. Students thus have an opportunity to discover and then rediscover, use and then re-use these basic strategies in all the poems they write on any subject.

■ **Meaning** We adopt here John Ciardi's observation that when reading and writing poetry, it's not *what* a poem means that's important, but *how* it means. The *what,* especially in deep and tender poems, means different things to different readers and is constantly unfolding as the poem is remembered and re-read. So the sourcebook doesn't put a lot of attention on the literal interpretation of poems. Rather, the emphasis is on *how* a poem acquires its meaning. The how is encompassed in the strategies poets use, as summarized above in *The Recursive Approach.*

Robert Frost

Setting Up a Poetry-Centered Classroom

■ **Reading Aloud** Lyric poetry is one of the easiest genres to inject into your classroom schedule, because the poems are usually *short.* Start and end the day by reading aloud a lyric poem *you* like. Ask students to guess why you like it, then invite them to give their own opinions about the poem. As your students acquire, through the sourcebook, the vocabulary to talk about poems (*form, metaphor, alliteration,* etc.), encourage them to use these terms as they talk about the poem.

■ **Students Reading Aloud** Make anthologies and other collections of poetry available in the classroom. (For suggestions, see the first idea on page 8 as well as the Bibliography on page 40.) Encourage kids to dip into these books to find poems they like, read them with a classmate, and then read them aloud to a larger group.

■ **Students Reading Their Own Poetry** You'll probably have some poetry buffs in your classroom who can either make up jingles at a moment's notice or who want to share right away some poem they've been working on and have finally finished. Let students know that you think poetry is important by adusting your regular curricular time-slots to allow for a a few minutes of spontaneous sharing.

E.E. Cummings

■ **Making Provisions for the Kids Who "Hate Poetry"** You might try directing these children to your collection of humorous poetry and folk rhymes. (See the Bibliography.) It's a rare child who doesn't get a chuckle out of a folk rhyme, a limerick, or a poem by Prelutsky or Silverstein. Invite these "poetry haters" to read their funny discoveries aloud to the class.

■ **Planning Some Long-range Poetry Projects** As your students get into poetry, many of them will like working on a lasting way of preserving and sharing their poems.

● **A Classroom Anthology** This is the most obvious and simplest way of collecting what students themselves consider to be the best of their work. The sourcebook encourages students to keep individual poetry portfolios. Out of this and the work students do in the Writing Lyric Poetry section, the class can compile and illustrate an anthology. Make copies of the anthology for students to take home, or to give to the school or community library and to other classrooms.

● **A Videotape Recording of a Poetry Reading** This requires some special steps that can engage every student. Here are the steps:

1. Ask each student to choose a favorite poem to read aloud. It can be the student's poem or a poem by someone else.

2. Have students work with a peer coach — a classmate who can suggest ways to make the reading most effective. Coaches should help readers concentrate on the questions such as the following:

What's the main feeling in this poem? Make your voice show the feeling.

What are the most important ideas and phrases in this poem? Stress them when you read aloud.

3. Provide practice time in a place where reader and coach can work together away from the rest of the class. Provide reader-coach teams with an audiotape to record readings until they find the one they like best.

4. After setting up the sequence in which readers will appear, present the entire poetry reading, and videotape it —perhaps with the help of a student-technician. An important aspect here is to often switch back and forth from the reader to the audience, to catch the audience's reaction to the poem.

5. Show the tape to the class. Ask students to look especially at the audience's reactions to poems. This is usually a very moving and insightful experience for both reader and listener, for it helps them to realize the profound effect good poetry has on us.

Emily Dickinson

Introducing Lyric Poetry

Here are a few activities and ideas to help you launch the study of lyric poetry:

■ Encourage serendipitous "dipping" into poetry by setting up groupings of poetry anthologies in different places in your classroom. Use the bibliography on page 40 for examples. For instance, you might keep poetry about animals and weather near your science center, general anthologies on a reading table, and poems by individual authors in your writing center. Distribute books of humorous poetry into the other categories.

■ Before students dip into the accompanying anthology, read aloud some poems from it or from the other poetry books in your classroom. Encourage students to discuss what they like, don't like, understand, or don't understand in these poems. This preview will give you an opportunity to informally check your students' attitudes about poetry in general, as well as their knowledge of the techniques and strategies poets use, providing you with an idea of what to concentrate on as your class studies lyric poetry.

■ Suggest that students make individual poetry portfolios and start using them right away. The portfolios can include poems they like that others have written, as well as their own ideas for poems, rough drafts of poems they'll be writing, copies of the activity sheets, and pictures they've found or drawn that inspire poems.

Page 9: Talking About The Lyric Part

You may wish to use this sheet as an all-class activity.

After students have decided on the pop song they want to work on, have them dictate the lines to you as you write them on the chalkboard; then have students copy the lines onto the activity sheet. Ask students to read the lines aloud to determine rhyming words and where the stress marks (/) should go to reflect the rhythm.

If there's disagreement about the *feeling* in the lyrics, encourage students to write their *own* ideas about what the feeling is.

Suggest that students make a brief list of the feelings they'd like to eventually write about, and ask them to put the list in their poetry portfolios.

Page 10: Guidelines For Reading Poetry

This page introduces students to the reading strategy they'll be using throughout the anthology: reading a poem aloud with a partner and discussing it. You may wish to work through this guideline model with the class as a whole, first reading the poem aloud yourself, then discussing the questions in the margin and writing other questions that arise for the last two stanzas.

Stress the mysteriousness of the image in Blake's poem: a tree that grows from anger and finally bears a poison fruit that destroys someone. Encourage students to relate the idea in this image to their own experiences with anger. Explain that most good poetry reminds readers of things they've seen, experiences they've had, or their own deep feelings.

Talking About The *Lyric* Part

The *lyrics,* or words, to music have qualities that make them different from the words in a fiction story or the words in a textbook paragraph. Lyrics and lyric poetry are meant to be said aloud or sung. With a partner or a group of classmates, investigate the lyrics to one of your favorite songs. Write a few lines from the song on the lines below.

_____

_____

_____

1. **Sounds:** In the lines you've written, underline any words that rhyme at the ends of lines. Then circle any words that come close together and begin with the same sound, like skit, scat; or wonder and wander.

2. **Rhythm:** When you say or sing lyrics, you stress certain words or syllables to capture the rhythm. Read your song lines aloud and put a stress mark (/) over the words or syllables you'd emphasize if you were singing them. Here's an example:

   /
   You can't be beat
   /
   If you know the street,
   /
   For the people there
   /
   Are just so aware!

3. **A Feeling:** Most lyrics convey a certain feeling. The feeling can be a simple one, like "I love my neighborhood." Or the feeling can be a mysterious and slightly hazy one, like "Who can tell me who I am?" On the lines below, write the feeling — simple or mysterious — that your song lyrics suggest to you.

_____

_____

* During this study, you'll be writing your own lyric poetry. With a partner, discuss some of the feelings you'd like to express in your poems.

INTRODUCING LYRIC POETRY

Guidelines For Reading Poetry

Poets play with words, often by compressing a lot of ideas together into a short form. The result is often a sort of word-puzzle. One of your main tasks is to solve these lyrical puzzles. Here's how:

1. **First read the poem aloud, alone or with a partner.** If there's no punctuation at the end of a line, just go on reading to the next line.

2. **As you read, note and discuss any questions you have about the poem.** For example:

A Poison Tree

I was angry with my friend.
I told my wrath, my wrath did end.
I was angry with my foe.
I told it not, my wrath did grow.

And I watered it in fears
Night and morning with my tears;
And I sunned it with my smiles
And with soft deceitful wiles.

What's *wrath?* Does it have something to do with anger?

I think a *foe's* the opposite of a *friend.* Let's check these words in the dictionary!

Oh! Now I'm beginning to understand the title of this poem. The poet is comparing his anger to a growing tree. I'll look up *deceitful* and *wiles,* though.

With a reading partner, read aloud and discuss the next parts of the poem.

And it grew both day and night
Till it bore an apple bright;
And my foe beheld it shine,
And he knew that it was mine.
And into my garden stole,
When the night had veiled the pole.(*)
In the morning glad I see
My foe outstretched below the tree.
                                                William Blake
(*) "Pole" means thePole Star or North Star

3. **Now that you've discussed the poem and answered your questions about it, read it aloud again.** This time, you'll probably read it with more expression and understanding. For example:

A. What does the poet say happens when you don't express your anger? _____

_____

B. In your opinion, what is the poison tree? _____

_____

Nature

Introducing The Section

Explain that the poems students will be reading have one thing in common: they're all about nature. In other ways, they are different: some rhyme, some don't; the poems express many different feelings; some poems seem easy to figure out, while others are more puzzling. You may wish to read aloud an example from the anthology of each of these. Remind students to read each poem aloud with a partner or small group, following the guidelines on page 10.

Page 12: A Preview

If you have a pair of binoculars or a camera with a zoom lens, invite students to use them to practice zeroing in on a detail of some natural object — a bird, a flower, a raindrop on the window pane, a leaf on a classroom plant — and then describe the details they saw that they didn't notice before.

Even without these magnifiers, you can get students to brainstorm a list of details about some natural object you display, such as a rock, a twig, or a fish in your aquarium. With these activities as a preamble, partners are better able to tell details about the items on the list. Invite partners to share their best observations by reading them aloud to the class. Remind students to save their completed activity sheet in their portfolios.

Page 13: Responding As A Reader

Use this page to help students appreciate the validity of their personal tastes in poetry. While the poem titles they list for categories 1 through 5 on the chart should be accurate examples of the category, the poems they choose as "best" for these categories and the poems they choose for categories 6 and 7 will express purely personal responses. Encourage reading partners to share and discuss their completed charts in a small group so that they can expand on and explain their choices and compare and contrast different responses. Ask students

to carry out the activity at the bottom of the page. They might set this response up in chart form, with the poem's title on the left and a sentence about what they'd like to try on the right.

Page 14: A Special Way Of Seeing

This activity gives students a beginning opportunity to explore imagery and a chance to apply the guidelines on page 10 to find out "how this poem works." Later in this sourcebook, students will have further opportunities to investigate imagery. After discussing the completed page with the class, ask students to do the activity at the bottom of the page.

Page 15: The Sounds Of Poetry

You may wish to use this page as a whole-class activity. Ask students to recall or review the sound elements of lyrics that they investigated on page 9, and explain that on this page they can get a closer look at what links lyric poetry with music.

Page 16: Getting Started On Your Own Nature Poetry

Most students will be quite ready by now to attempt a nature poem of their own. To encourage them to write first about something "small," ask them to recall the "zoom lens" activity they did as preface to page 12. For poetry ideas, suggest that they review the descriptions they wrote on that page as well as the ideas they've jotted down in their portfolios.

Page 17: Playing With Your Poem

Emphasize the play-and-practice thrust of this activity. Some students may wish to read their completed poems aloud to the class or to a small group. Others may wish to work on them some more before sharing them.

LYRIC POETRY ABOUT NATURE

A Preview

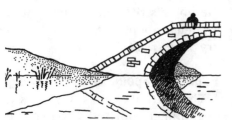

"Nature" is a very big topic. It includes all the living things around us: from the stupendous — such as a gray whale — to the tiny— such as a blade of grass. "Nature" also includes nonliving things, such as wind, stars, oceans, and mountains; and events, such as the first snowfall or the arrival of spring.

Lyric poets don't try to tell you everything about a natural object or event. Instead, poets tell carefully about small details they've observed. As a poet, imagine that you have a built-in zoom lens, like the zoom lens on a camera. With this powerful lens, you can zero in for a new, close look at details about some everyday, ordinary natural thing. Then, instead of snapping a close-up photo, you write a close-up poem.

With a partner, discuss some simple observations you've made about each natural thing listed below. Write one of your observations on the line.

1. Snow falling _____

_____

2. Moonlight _____

_____

3. A pet cat _____

_____

4. A windy day _____

_____

5. Grass _____

_____

* Underline the words or phrases you like best above. Save them in your portfolio as ideas for your own poems.

LYRIC POETRY ABOUT NATURE

Responding As A Reader

Read the poems in this section aloud with your partner. Follow the guidelines from page 10. As you read, find some poems that fit into each of the following categories. Then decide which *one* in that category you both like best. It's OK to disagree. Make notes about any disagreements in column 3 on the chart.

CATEGORIES	BEST POEM IN THIS CATEGORY	DISAGREEMENTS
1. Poems with obvious rhyme and rhythm		
2. Poems that repeat phrases over and over		
3. Poems that don't have rhymes at the ends of lines		
4. Poems that have humor in them		
5. Poems that contrast or compare things in unusual ways		
6. Poems that express an idea that really gets to me!		
7. Poems that give me that "light-bulb" experience: "Wow! I never thought of it that way before!		

* **Responding as a Writer:** What poem or poems in this section are your personal favorites? In *your* personal portfolio, write the poems' titles. Tell what the poet does that you'd like to try in your own poetry.

LYRIC POETRY ABOUT NATURE

A Special Way Of Seeing

Some poems about nature are easy to understand. For example, in the Paiute poem "The Grass on the Mountain" (page 18 in your anthology), the speaker gives you a vivid, zoom-lens picture of a cold and dreary winter.

Some nature poems are a little more puzzling. An example is "Dancing" (page 20 in your anthology). Exactly who or what is dancing in this poem? With a partner, use the guidelines on page 10 to read and discuss the poem. Then answer these questions about it.

1. Are there any humans mentioned in this poem?_____

2. What natural things *are* mentioned in it?_____

3. What are the action words, or verbs, in the poem? For example, *sway* and *floating* are two of them. _____

4. Judging from the action words, what's the weather like in the poem? _____

5. Who *are* the dancers in "Dancing"?_____

6. The first line of the poem mentions "wide sleeves." When you first read the word sleeves, of course, you think of a human being in a wide-sleeved garment. Look at the picture below. What are these "wide sleeves" really?_____

   Why do "sweet scents" come from them? _____

*Responding as a writer: In your portfolio, jot down some lines to show a scene in which nonhuman things in nature seem to be performing a human action, such as talking, arguing, laughing, or rushing.

Name (s) _____

The Sounds Of Poetry

Recall that lyric poetry has a song-like quality to it. You've probably found that song-like quality as you've read nature poems aloud with you partner. Here's a chance to review and add to your understanding of sounds that make songs.

1. **Rhyme: Ending sounds** Rhyming words at the end of lines are the easiest way to make song-sounds. Some poets make every other line end with rhyming words. Re-read "April" (anthology page 7) and write the end-rhyme words in each stanza:

Stanza 1, lines 2 and 4: _____

Stanza 2, lines 2 and 4: _____

2. **Alliteration: Beginning sounds** Poets often get a musical quality by putting words close together that *begin* with the same sound. Here are some examples from your anthology:

- "Slowly, silently...."
- "..snuffs and sniffs,"
- " Lotus lilies....."
- " ...dark and deep"
- "...bicycle bell"
- "...plum tree petals..."

With a partner, find and write some other examples of alliteration from poems in the anthology.

_____

_____

3. **Repetition** As in a song, a poem often has repeated phrases. For example, Walt Whitman's poem (anthology page 22) repeats *"Give me..."* at the beginning of each line. With your partner, find and write the repeated phrases in these poems:

- "April Rain Song," by Langston Hughes (anthology page 6)

_____

_____

- "My Little Birds" (anthology page 19)

_____

_____

LYRIC POETRY ABOUT NATURE

Getting Started On Your Own Nature Poetry

As a poet writing about nature, you'll be dealing with two main things:

1. **Your inspiration.** Something in nature grabs your attention all of a sudden. You yearn to tell about it.

2. **The words you'll use.** Remember that a poem is a word snapshot, with your observations and feelings pared down into the bare essentials for your readers.

Use the chart below to help you plan your poem about nature. Examples are given at the top of the chart to help you get started. Add to the chart your own ideas about *your* inspiration from nature. Refer to your ideas on page 12.

MY INSPIRATION (THE BIG IDEA)	LET'S NARROW THAT IDEA DOWN A LITTLE!	WORDS AND PHRASES THAT COME TO MIND
(EXAMPLE) Birds in a snowstorm. They're all taking off for somewhere.	I wonder where birds go in a snowstorm. Do they hide? If so, where	bundled in bushes; nestling in window sills and roofs; startled by snowflakes wind whips wings
(YOUR TURN!)		

LYRIC POETRY ABOUT NATURE

Playing With Your Poem

On page 16, you wrote some basic ideas for your poem about nature. On the lines below, play and practice as you write a first draft of your poem. Poets are always changing things, so use a pencil with a big eraser! Here are some guidelines to help you as you play and practice.

- Poems don't have to rhyme.
- Poems *do* have musical qualities in them. See page 15 for some ideas about how to choose and juggle words to make them sound musical.
- Poems are meant to be read aloud with a certain *rhythm.* Play around with the lines of your poem. Start and end them so that when you're reading them aloud they have the rhythm you want.
- Check this draft of your poem with a reading partner who'll read your poem aloud to you. Then make any changes you think will make your poem more musical.
- Be sure to put this poem in your portfolio when you're finished.

_____
_____
_____
_____
_____
_____
_____
_____
_____
_____
_____
_____

People

Introducing The Section

Review the ways in which students used the skill of *observation* to help them write poems about nature. Then invite the class to brainstorm how they could use the same skill to write poems about people. What *details* could they focus on? Examples are: the way a person moves; his or her general appearance; some behavior or attitude that affects other people; something unusual about the person; something funny the person does. Read aloud a couple of poems from the anthology to illustrate particular aspects of human beings that poets find interesting.

Page 19: People In Song Lyrics

You might help students get started on this page by first asking the class to brainstorm a list of popular songs that tell about people. Suggest that partners refer to the list for ideas as they do the first activity. Ask students to keep the predictions they write for activity 2 so they can check them after reading the poems.

Page 20: Readers' Responses

Suggest that partners share their finished charts with a group of classmates and compare and contrast their results. Encourage students to tell *why* they like the "favorite phrases" in the third column on the chart. Remind your writers to add their list of personal favorites to their portfolios.

Page 21: Exploring Forms

You may wish to work through the page with the whole class to make sure all students grasp the basic distinction between traditional rhymed, rhythmical poetry and poetry written to capture the sound of natural speech patterns. You'll be entering here the whole question of "What makes it a poem if it doesn't rhyme?" Emphasize that poetry is not just rhyme, but the sound of the lines as you read them aloud. Ask volunteers to find and read examples of other poems in this section and in the Nature section that don't have a regular rhythm and rhyme, but do capture the way people sound when they talk.

Page 22: Oh, Those Word Pictures!

This activity and the next one (page 23) delve into the heart of poetry: imagery. Students now have an opportunity to learn how imagery "works," how it's constructed, so that they can not only talk about it concisely as they discuss poetry, but also *use* it with awareness as they *write* poetry. You may wish to introduce the page by discussing how we use comparisons in our everyday talk, as in "I'm tired as a horse," "She's as playful as a kitten," "He's a regular machine when he does his homework."

Page 23: Making All The World Seem Human

Introduce the activity by discussing some of the ways nonhuman things often seem human to very young children. For example, autumn leaves blowing across a lawn may seem to be "chasing" you, or a rock might seem to be staring at you. Encourage students to brainstorm other examples, and write these on poster paper for students to use as a reference when they write their own poems. After partners have completed the first activity, bring the class together again to discuss responses. Encourage individual students to share the poems they write for the second activity before putting the poems in their portfolios.

Page 24: Writing More Poetry Of Your Own

Suggest that students work with a partner on this activity. With a "partner-poem," students have a chance to use the guidelines on page 10 in a slightly new way: to *build* a poem together, and then analyze what they've built. Invite partners to read their poem aloud to the class.

LYRIC POETRY ABOUT PEOPLE

Preview: People In Song Lyrics

There are many songs that tell about particular people. The lyric-writer zooms in on a character or characters and writes a brief, rhythmic description of them. As a listener, you come away with a distinct, vivid impression of what the character is like. For example, the lyrics may emphasize that the character is sad; or a good friend; or beautiful but unkind; or mysterious; or in trouble; or brave.

1. Below, list the titles of three songs about people. Then, write the name of the person. (In some songs, the person is just referred to as "you.") In the right-hand column, write a brief phrase that gives your general impression of the person.

SONG TITLE	PERSON'S NAME	MY IMPRESSION OF THE PERSON
A.		
B.		
C.		

2. Listed below are three different characters. Quickly brainstorm and write the impression or mental image you get of each.

A. A young girl who likes to scare people with snakes she finds _____

B. A cowboy driving cattle across a Western range _____

C. A woman who does her gardening at night _____

*The characters listed in 2, above, appear in poems you'll read next in your anthology. As you read, look for the words and phrases the poets use to build your impressions of these and other characters.

LYRIC POETRY ABOUT PEOPLE

Readers' Responses

Read the poems in this section aloud with your partner. Follow the guidelines on page 10. As you read, find poetry characters that fit into the following categories and list the titles of the poems. (It's OK to list a poem in more than one category.) In the last column, write some favorite phrases from the poems that you and your partner like especially well.

CATEGORIES	POEM TITLES	FAVORITE PHRASES
Characters who make us laugh		
Characters we admire		
Characters we don't like		
Characters who remind us of real people we know		

* **A Writer's Response:** What poem or poems in this section are *your* personal favorites? In your portfolio, write the poems' titles. Tell what the poet does that you'd like to try in your own poetry.

Exploring Forms

Poetry is meant to be *heard,* not just read silently. Poets know this, and set up the lines of their poems accordingly.

1. Some poets set up lines so that their poem has a constant rhythm and rhyme. Here's an example. Read it aloud to stress the accent marks (/) and the rhyming words (underlined).

>   /   /   /
> But when you're with some other ones,
>   /   /   /
> You feel so tired <u>inside,</u>
>   /   /   /
> Your thoughts begin to shrivel up
>   /   /   /
> Like leaves all brown and <u>dried.</u>

In your anthology, find two other poems that use this constant rhythm and rhyme system. Write the titles of the poems.

_____

_____

2. Some poets set up lines to show the natural pauses people make when they're speaking. Read the following example. Pause ever-so-slightly at the end of each line to make your speech sound natural.

> He made a mountain
> And a green tree
> And small rocks
> And smaller rocks

In your anthology, find two other poems that use this natural-speech-pattern approach. Write the titles of the poems.

_____

* **A Writer's Response:** Refer to your portfolio and review the poems you've selected as your personal favorites so far. Write *rhythm and rhyme* or *natural speech pattern* to show the method the poet used. Put a star (*) next to the method you'd like to try when you write a lyric poem about a person.

Oh, Those Word Pictures!

Recall that poets are like photographers with zoom lenses. They work to create vivid word pictures of their subjects. Here are two of the picture-making strategies they use:

1. **Simile:** Using "like" or "as" in a comparison. In your anthology, the poem "my friend" uses many similes. Examples are underlined below:

he <u>cools</u>   his <u>voice</u>

like <u>water</u>   is ready

in the hot <u>noon</u> **as** <u>a spring bird</u>

Find and write the similes from the following anthology poems.

A. "Some People" (anthology page 28) stanza 1: _____

_____

B. "Fisherman" (anthology page 23) lines 2 and 3: _____

_____

"Fisherman," lines 11 and 12: _____

_____

C. "Portrait by a Neighbour" (anthology page 27) stanza 4: _____

_____

2. **Metaphor:** Making a comparison without "like" or "as." Reread the third stanza of "Snake woman" (anthology page 37). What's being compared to "this vein of cool green metal" or to "a raw bracelet gripping my wrist"? _____

Does the poet use "like" or "as" in these comparisons?

Look back at the poem "Fisherman". List some metaphors you find in it.

_____

* On a separate sheet of paper, practice building similes and metaphors. Choose a person in your neighborhood or an animal you like. Use a simile and then a metaphor to describe each one. Save your comparisons for possible use in one of your poems.

LYRIC POETRY ABOUT PEOPLE

Making All The World Seem Human

Poets can not only make human characters seem vivid, they can also make nonhuman things seem like people. Poets do this by using a strategy called *personification*. Personification gives human qualities to things that aren't human. For example, in the third stanza of "Portrait by a Neighbour," the poet calls the lettuce "lazy." Vegetables can't scientifically be called "lazy," because that's a human trait. But "lazy lettuce" is great in a poem, because it gives a vivid picture of a plant that grows pretty slowly.

1. Read these examples of personification from the nature poems in your anthology. With a

partner, discuss *why* they are personification.

A. "Let the rain <u>kiss</u> you." _____

B. "The snow <u>has possessed</u> the mountain." _____

C. "When the hurricane unfolds

<u>Its fierce accordion of winds</u>,

<u>On the tips of its toes</u>,

<u>Agile dancer, it sweeps whirling</u>...."

_____

2. Use the lines below for practice. From the observations you made about nature on page 12,

choose the one you like best. Write a few lines in which you use personification to make the

nonhuman thing seem human in some way.

_____

_____

_____

_____

_____

LYRIC POETRY ABOUT PEOPLE

Writing More Poetry Of Your Own

Take some time to practice a few of the techniques poets use.

1. First, find or think of a scene in which a person is involved in some way with the rest of nature. Write a sentence or phrase to identify your subject. _____

_____

2. Build your phrase or sentence into a brief poem, using some of the techniques you've learned. Remember to work with a pencil, in case you want to change things.

_____

_____

_____

_____

_____

_____

_____

_____

3. Re-read your poem to see if you've included at least one of these strategies for comparing things.

_____metaphor   _____simile   _____personification

4. Which of these "sound" strategies did you use? (Review p. 15)

_____ rhymes at the end of lines

_____ alliteration

_____ repetition

* Read your poem aloud, or listen to a partner read it. Make any changes you wish in your poem. You'll have a chance to change it later, too. Then put your poem in your portfolio along with the lyric poem you wrote on page 17.

Thoughts
And Feelings

Introducing The Section

Discuss different ways we express our feelings. Take a strong feeling like *anger* as an example. We can express it by acting angry or speaking angrily; we can talk about our anger; or we can write about our anger. Remind students that William Blake used the last device — writing — in the poem "A Poison Tree." Explain that in this section of the anthology students will read poems in which a wide variety of feelings are expressed.

Page 26: Concentrating On The Mind Of The Poet

Discuss the opening paragraph on this page with the class. Invite volunteers to find in the anthology poems about nature and poems about people in which they can detect the poet's thoughts and feelings about the subject. After discussing the next paragraph, suggest that students do the activity independently. (This will encourage students to be truly personal and candid about their reactions to the items in the list.) If they wish, students can compare results with a partner. After students have circled the subject they'd like to write about, ask them to put the page in their portfolios to use as an idea source.

Page 27: Readers' Responses

Encourage partners to use the page 10 guidelines as they read the poems in this section. Review the directions on this page to make sure students understand them: they'll select the poem or poems in each category that they think fit.

Page 28: A Very Odd Form Indeed!

In this activity, students make an initial foray into *free verse.* Since free verse is common in modern poetry, you might want to discuss the term: free verse cuts *free* of the ordinary standards for setting up poems in stanzas, using rhyme, or even arranging lines in natural speech patterns. Instead, the lines are arranged to reflect the way the *feelings, thoughts,* and *observations* "hop around" in the poet's mind.

Read through and discuss the first part of the page with the class and discuss the first part of Cummings's poem and the accompanying notes. Ask partners to carry out the first activity, then compare their responses with classmates. Emphasize that even "free poetry" has rules that the poet sets. In this poem, Cummings's "rule" for himself was that all the lines should show the hippy-hoppy actions and talk and sounds of people being happy on a "Just-spring" day. Ask students to carry out the second activity independently. Supply lots of extra paper so that your poets can experiment freely.

Page 29: Would You Like To Leave A Message?

Use this page to help students understand that in most lyric poetry, the very last thing poets have on their mind is *teaching* someone something. Read and discuss the introductory paragraph with the class, and suggest that partners carry out the first activity together, then compare and discuss their results with classmates.

Partners can then continue with the second activity.

Page 30: Continuing With Your Own Poetry

Go over the introductory paragraph and the sample poem with the class. Encourage students to carry out the two activities on their own. Ask students to keep their rough drafts out for use on page 31.

Page 31: Some Say A Poem Is Never Finished

Discuss the opening paragraphs with the class. Suggest that students work with a writing partner as they analyze the drafts they wrote on page 30 and consider how to change them. Then invite small groups of students to get together and discuss what they learned about poetry by revising it. Students may wish to read their poems aloud before putting them in their portfolios.

LYRIC POETRY ABOUT THOUGHTS AND FEELINGS

Concentrating On The Mind Of The Poet

Every good poem describing nature or people in the outside world also gives you a glimpse of what the poet is thinking and feeling. For example, in the nature poem "Dancing" you catch the poet's thought that in a gentle wind, flowers, clouds, and water seem to move together in a dance. You also catch the poet's feeling of awe at the beauty of this sight.

Often, however, poets want to *concentrate* on their inner thoughts and feelings. The thought or feeling becomes the subject of the poem. To preview this section, write a thought or feeling you have on each of the following subjects:

1. Too much noise around you! _____

_____

2. A favorite book _____

_____

3. Beauty _____

_____

4. Heroic people _____

_____

5. Graveyards _____

_____

  * Circle the numeral of the subject above you'd like best to write about in your own poem. Then read on to see what other poets have revealed about their thoughts and feelings on these and other subjects.

LYRIC POETRY ABOUT THOUGHTS AND FEELINGS

Readers' Responses

Read the poems in this section of the anthology aloud with a partner. Follow the guidelines on page 10. As you read, identify the poems described below. Write the title or titles in the space provided on the chart. You may not want to include all the poems in this section. Also, you may decide that some poem titles fit into more than one category.

DESCRIPTION	TITLE OR TITLES
A feeling of fear is treated humorously.	
A feeling of anxiety is treated honestly.	
Thoughts about the wonder of life are expressed very seriously.	
Thoughts about the wonder of life are expressed in a happy-go-lucky way.	
Feeling and thoughts about the purpose and meaning of my life will always be with me.	

*A Writer's Response: What poem or poems in this section are your personal favorites? In your portfolio, write the poems' titles. Tell what the poet does that you'd like to try in your own poetry.

A Very Odd Form Indeed!

If E. E. Cummings's poem "in Just-" gave you some trouble, join the group! Cummings is the superstar of playful poets, of odd forms and of words all run together. He set up the lines of his poems the way he did to capture a *feeling of playfulness*. And when he couldn't think of an existing word to convey his thought, why, he'd playfully make up a new one! Re-read the beginning of the poem below, and talk about the notes to the right of it.

in Just- spring   when the world is mud- luscious the little lame balloonman whistles   far and wee

Well, who cares about the exact date? It's Just-spring! And there's no other good word for the squishiness of mud, except "mud-luscious."

Now, a whistle comes through the air in a long sort of way, so I'll space the words far apart to show that sound.

1. With a partner, read the rest of the poem to find examples of how the poet did the things listed below in his poem. Write your discoveries and examples on a separate sheet of paper.

   A. Showed how we often run words together when we're talking.
   B. Made the lines of the poem look like the *jumping* and *hopping* games kids play in "Just-spring."
   C. Made the balloonman's whistle seem like it was fading into the distance.

2. On a separate piece of paper experiment with writing a poem of your own in a form that's like a picture of the thoughts and ideas in it.

   A. Choose a completed poem from your portfolio, or some lines of poetry you're just beginning to work on.
   B. Think about the feeling in your poem. Is it a sad feeling? an angry one? a happy one?
   C. Arrange the lines of your poetry to show the feeling. Also, you can write some words big, little, or in capitals to convey your feeling. Anything goes! This is *your* experiment!

LYRIC POETRY ABOUT THOUGHTS AND FEELINGS

Would You Like To Leave a Message?

Most good poets don't start out thinking, "Well, I think I'll write a poem that has a little lesson or moral in it for my readers." Yet somehow, when you write a good poem your readers *do* come away from it thinking, "I *learned* something!"—perhaps a new way of looking at nature, people, or human thoughts and feelings.

1. Re-read the following poems in your anthology, and write what *you* learned by reading and studying them. Remember that because poetry is a mysterious and wonderful puzzle, you may find several messages in a single poem. Remember, too, that the message *you* find may be quite different from the one your classmate finds.

    A. "A Song of Greatness" (anthology page 48) _____

    _____

    B. "Leisure" (anthology page 51) _____

    _____

2. Here's a word to wise poets: Never begin with a lesson or message in mind. Just write truly and vividly about what you see, feel, and think. Leave it to your readers to discover messages, lessons, or meanings in your poem.

    A. To test this advice, exchange a poem of yours with a partner. Read your partner's poem and write what you learned from it.

    _____

    _____

    B. With your partner, discuss the "messages" you discovered in each other's poems. Were you surprised by what your partner found? Write what your partner found in your poem that's a surprise to you.

    _____

    _____

LYRIC POETRY ABOUT THOUGHTS AND FEELINGS

Continuing With Your Own Poetry

Because you're human, you're always having thoughts and feelings. Even if you're slumped back there in your chair thinking "I have absolutely no thoughts right now," or "I'm feeling absolutely nothing," you can write about having *no* thoughts and *no* feelings. Here's an example:

Dry as bone, my mind's all alone.
No thoughts about a friend,
No FEELING.
Just me staring at the ceiling.
Will this ever end?
Or will I have a GREAT THOUGHT?
And come round the bend again
To SHARING again?

1. Or maybe you're full of a lot of thoughts and feelings about one of the following subjects (Check one or two that apply to you now.)

   ☐ weather

   ☐ something you heard today in a news report

   ☐ a fight or argument   ☐ a school situation   ☐ a problem with a friend

   ☐ an animal I care about   ☐ a dream or plan I have   ☐ a neighbor I worry about

2. On the lines below, write a draft of a poem about one of the subjects above, or about another thought or feeling that occupies your attention at this moment.

_____

_____

_____

_____

_____

Some Say a Poem Is Never Finished

A poem about your feelings is very personal, almost like a diary entry. Because the poem belongs to *you* especially, you may want to keep going back and changing it. Some poets even seek *perfection*! For example, William Butler Yeats achieved great fame with his poetry. Yet even after his poems won prizes, he'd change them. In a few of his poems, he was making changes 25 years after they were published!

So, feel free to make changes in the poem you wrote for page 30! Re-read your poem and figure out ways to improve it.

Here are things to look for; Check the strategies you've used. Cross out the ones you don't want to try. Circle the ones you'd *like* to try when you revise your poem.

A. Strategies with sound:

☐ a regular rhythm   ☐ rhymes at the end of some lines

☐ alliteration   ☐ repetition

B. Strategies with form:

☐ lines that are written to show a musical rhythm

☐ lines that imitate human speech patterns

☐ lines that are arranged to show the feeling and idea of a poem, like E.E. Cummings' "in Just-"

C. Strategies for comparing things:

☐ metaphor   ☐ simile   ☐ personification

* On a separate sheet of paper, write another draft of your poem from page 30. Make any changes you want to make, using your checklist above as a guide. Put your new draft of your poem in your portfolio.

Analyzing Lyric Poetry

This section is designed to help students compare and contrast the different poems they've read so that they can synthesize and apply their understanding about what makes a poem a poem.

Page 33: Readers' Responses: Your Favorites

This page helps students reinforce the concept that lyric poems (1) express or evoke a feeling or thought; and (2) use distinctly poetic strategies to pull it off. Go over the introductory paragraph with the class and ask students to carry out the activity independently. Set aside a classroom period for discussing the results. Then have students summarize the discussion by telling what they learned from it about poetry and about how tastes in poetry vary.

Page 34: Evaluating Different Forms

You may wish to have student partners work on this activity together. Partners may have different responses to the questions in the first and second columns on the chart; encourage them to note their areas of disagreement. The first column calls for "correct" answers: "A Baby's Feet" has distinct rhythm and rhyme, "You better be ready" follows a natural speech pattern, and "In Quiet Night" is playful (free verse). In the discussion suggested at the bottom of the page, students should be able to point out the characteristics of the poems that helped them categorize them.

Page 35: Searching For Sounds And Pictures

Suggest that students review their work on pages 15, 21, 22, and 23 before they undertake this activity. Responses here will vary widely, as the anthology has many examples of each strategy.

Page 36: Thoughts And Feelings Everywhere!

This page builds on the concept developed on page 33: that images, feelings, and thoughts are present in all good lyric poetry. Partners may wish to complete the activity together, then share their decisions with a small group of classmates. This group might present their awards before the class by reading what they've written in each ribbon, then reading the poetry lines that inspired their choice.

Page 37: Why Is It A Poem?

This page provides another way for students to discriminate the differences between prose and poetry. The poems referred to are:

1. "my friend (page 32); 2. "Silver" (page 13); 3. "Books Fall Open" (page 40). As for why these are poems, students might cite the abundant use of metaphor in "my friend," the use of rhyme, rhythm, alliteration, and personification in "Silver," and the rhyme and natural speech patterns in "Books Fall Open, " along with the abundant use of alliteration in the last four lines of this poem. Some students may also call attention to the "feeling" quality of the poems, which is absent from the prose re-tellings. Consider making the final activity on the page the basis for a class game.

Page 38: Explaining What You Know

You might set this up in the form of a debate. After students have written their answers to the three remarks and collected refuting examples, ask partners to act out the parts of the skeptic who knows little about poetry and the knowledgeable person who does know something. Have the debaters expand on their points of view, and encourage the "knowledgeable" debater to use several examples to make points.

Name (s) _____

Readers' Responses: Your Favorites

The poetry anthology you've been reading is divided into three sections: nature; people; and thoughts and feelings. From each section, choose the poem you like best and write the title in column 1 on the chart. In column 2, tell what feelings or ideas this poem gave you. In column 3, identify a special poetry strategy the writer used that you especially admire.

(Use the checklist on page 31 to help you find the exact term for the strategy.) In column 4 , give a precise example of the strategy from the poem.

1. MY FAVORITE POEM IN THIS SECTION	2. FEELING OR IDEA I GET FROM THIS POEM	3. STRATEGY I ADMIRE IN THIS POEM	4. EXAMPLE OF THE STRATEGY
Nature My favorite is:			
People My favorite is:			
Thoughts and Feelings My favorite is:			

Evaluating Different Forms

The poems you've been reading have different forms. Some poems have a distinct rhyme and rhythm pattern, as you'd find in song lyrics. Others show natural pauses in speaking. A few have lines set up playfully, to capture the feeling in the poem. Write the following titles in the categories where they belong. Then fill in the other column with *your* personal responses about the form.

"In Quiet Night"   **"A Baby's Feet"**   **"You better be ready"**

FORM	IS THIS FORM EASY OR DIFFICULT TO READ? EXPLAIN.	DO YOU LIKE TO WRITE IN THIS FORM? WHY, OR WHY NOT?
Distinct rhythm and rhyme:		
Natural speech pattern:		
Playful, to show feeling in poem:		

* Discuss your completed chart with a group of classmates. Explain how you chose the title for each category in the left hand column. Share more about the ideas you wrote in the other two columns.

ANALYZING LYRIC POETRY

Searching For Sounds And Pictures

Use your anthology to find lines or phrases that are examples of the strategies named in the circles. Write the example.

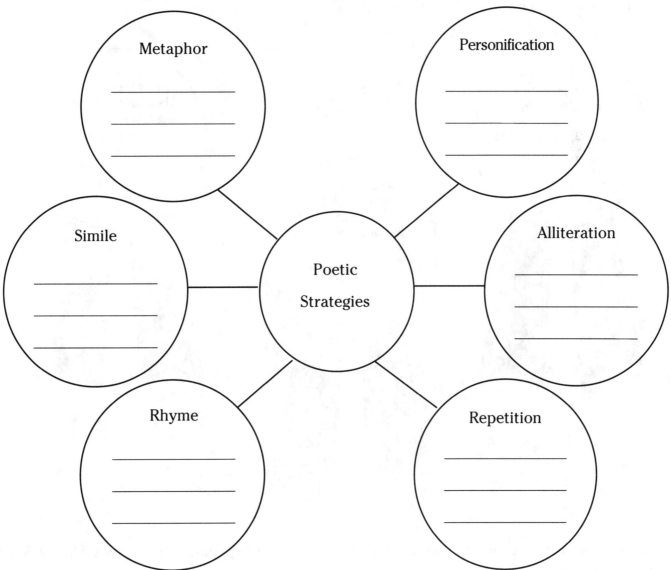

Metaphor

_____
_____
_____

Personification

_____
_____
_____

Simile

_____
_____
_____

Poetic

Strategies

Alliteration

_____
_____
_____

Rhyme

_____
_____
_____

Repetition

_____
_____
_____

* Discuss your examples with some classmates to see if they agree. As a game, ask your classmates to recall or find the title of the poems from which your examples come.

ANALYZING LYRIC POETRY

Thoughts And Feelings Everywhere!

As you know, every good poem gives you a distinct feeling or helps you to see an ordinary thing in a whole new way. Make your awards for the prizes named in the ribbons below. Write the poem's title and your reasons for choosing the poem.

Award to a Poem About Nature that made me feel grateful:

_____

_____

Award to a Poem About People that made me think about different points of view:

_____

_____

Award to a Poem About Thoughts and Feelings that helped me appreciate simple things in nature

_____

_____

* Discuss your awards with a classmate. Read lines from the poems aloud to give examples of why you chose them.

ANALYZING LYRIC POETRY

Why Is It A Poem?

This is a question that will always be unfolding for you. To discover some of your own answers, read the sentences at the left, then find the poem in your anthology that matches it. Write the title of the poem, then give your ideas about why it *is* a poem.

PARAGRAPH	POEM TITLE	WHY IT'S A POEM
My friend is always there for me. When I'm sad, he cheers me up. When I'm angry, he calms me down.		
I read a lot of books. I'm always looking for books that tell me something I don't already know!		
Sometimes I walk around at night and look at the moonlight. It's great! Moonlight lights up all sorts of things!		

* Find another poem in your anthology and translate it into a few sentences. Ask a classmate to find the matching poem and explain why it *is* poetry.

ANALYZING LYRIC POETRY

Explaining What You Know

Imagine that you're having a discussion with someone who doesn't know as much as about poetry as you do now. This imaginary person's remarks are given below. Answer each remark with your own ideas and knowledge about poetry. At the end of each answer, refer to a poem in the anthology.

1. **Poetry is just a lot of words put together so they rhyme.** *Your response:* _____

_____

_____

_____

See this poem in the anthology: _____

2. **Poetry hasn't got anything to tell me that I don't already know.** *Your response:* _____

_____

_____

_____

See this poem in the anthology: _____

3. **Poetry is always about things like flowers and raindrops.** *Your response:* _____

_____

_____

_____

See this poem in the anthology: _____

 * Suppose this imaginary person says, "Poetry is easy to write." On the basis of your writing experience, do you agree or disagree? Discuss your response with a classmate.

Across The Curriculum

SOCIAL STUDIES

■ Write poems about places being studied.

■ Read poems from different American cultures and from other areas of the world.

■ Find poetic place names on a U.S. map. Use them in a poem.

MATH

■ Find or create ways of "measuring" poems.

■ Relate meter in poetry to math concepts about time.

■ Write math word problems in poetry form.

SCIENCE

■ On field trips, observe carefully and translate some notes into poetry.

■ Discuss: the "truth" in science and the "truth" in poems.

■ Find and share poems on subjects being studied.

Lyric Poetry

CRITICAL THINKING

■ When does prose sound like poetry?

■ Is poetry important in the world today?

CONTROVERSIES

■ different tastes in poetry

■ poems that don't seem like poems

ARTS

■ Set poems to music; write words to go with instrumental music.

■ Paint pictures of what poems bring to mind; use art to get ideas for poems.

■ Make an album of close-up photos or videotapes of subjects to use in poems.

■ Choreograph a selection of poems.

Recommended Books And Other Resources

GENERAL ANTHOLOGIES

Arbuthnot, May Hill, comp. *Time for Poetry*. Scott, Foresman, 1968.

Cole, Joannna, comp. *A New Treasury of Children's Poetry* Doubleday, 1984.

Hopkins, Lee Bennet and Misha Arenstein, comps. *Thread One to a Star*. Four Winds, 1976.

Kennedy, X.J., comp. *Knock at a Star*. Little, Brown 1985.

Koch, Kenneth and Kate Farrell, comps. *Talking to the Sun*. Holt, 1985.

Larrick, Nancy, comp. *Piping Down the Valleys Wild*. Delacorte, 1985.

Lewis, Richard, ed. *Miracles: Poems by Children of the English-Speaking World*. Publishing Center for Cultural Resources, 1966.

Moore, Lilian, comp. *Go With the Poem*. McGraw-Hill, 1979.

Untermeyer, Louis, comp. *The Golden Treasury of Poetry*. Golden Press, 1959.

SPECIAL SUBJECTS

Agree, Rose H., comp. *How To Eat a Poem and Other Morsels*. Pantheon, 1967. (FOOD POEMS)

Cole, William, comp. *Good Dog Poems*. Scribner, 1981.

Cole, William, comp. *The Poetry of Horses*. Scribner, 1979.

Eliot, T.S. *Old Possum's Book of Practical Cats*. Harcourt, 1982.

Fleischmann, Paul. *Joyful Noise: Poems for Two Voices*. Harper & Row, 1988.(POEMS ABOUT INSECTS) Meant to be read aloud by two voices. Newbery Medal

Hopkins, Lee Bennett, comp. *Click, Rumble, Roar: Poems About Machines*. Crowell, 1987.

Hopkins, Lee Bennet, comp. *Dinosaurs*. Harcourt, 1987.

Hopkins, Lee Bennet, comp. *Moments: Poems About the Seasons*. Harcourt, 1980.

Livingston, Myra Cohn, comp. *If the Owl Calls Again. Macmillan, 1990.*

Ness, Evaline, comp. Amelia Mixed the Mustard and other Poems. *Scribner, 1975.* (POEMS ABOUT INDEPENDENT-MINDED WOMEN)

Schwartz, Alvin, comp. *And the Green Grass Grew All Around*. HarperCollins, 1992. (FOLK POETRY.)

Yolen, Jane, comp. *Street Rhymes Around the World.* Wordsong/ Boyds Mill Press, 1992.

OUTSTANDING COLLECTIONS OF POEMS BY A SINGLE AUTHOR

Bryan, Ashley. *Sing to the Sun.* HarperCollins, 1992.

Chandra, Deborah. *Balloons and Other Poems.* Farrar, 1990.

Greenfield, Eloise. *Honey, I Love.* Crowell, 1978; and *Night on Neighborhood Street*. Dial, 1991.

Hughes, Langston. *Don't You Turn Back.* Knopf, 1969.

Mizamura, Kazue. *Flower Moon Snow: A Book of Haiku.* Crowell, 1977.

Peck, Robert Newton. *Bee Tree and Other Stuff.* Walker, 1975.

Rylant, Cynthia. *Waiting To Waltz: A Childhood.* Bradbury, 1984.

Sandburg, Carl. *Rainbows Are Made.* Harcourt, 1982.

Starbird, Kaye. *The Covered Bridge House and Other Poems.* Four Winds, 1979.

Worth, Valerie. *Small Poems.* Farrar, 1972. The three others are *More Small Poems* (1976), *Still More Small Poems* (1978),and *Small Poems Again* (1986). These are short gems of poems about everyday objects.

HUMOR

Bodecker, N.M. *A Person from Britain Whose Head Was the Shape of a Mitten and Other Limericks.* Atheneum, 1980.

Brewton, John E. and Lorraine Blackburn, comps.*They've Discovered A Head in the Box for the Bread: And Other Laughable Limericks.* Crowell, 1978.

Brewton, Sara and John E. Brewton, comps. *Shrieks at Midnight: Macabre Poems, Eerie and Humorous.* Crowell, 1969.

Ciardi, John. *Fast and Slow: Poems for Advanced Children and Beginning Parents.* Houghton Mifflin, 1975.

Ciardi, John. *The Hopeful Trout and Other Limericks.* Houghton Mifflin, 1989.

Cole, William, comp. *Beastly Boys and Ghastly Girls.* Dell, 1977.

Prelutsky, Jack, comp. *For Laughing Out Loud: Poems To Tickle Your Funnybone.* Knopf, 1991

Prelutsky,Jack. *The New Kid on the Block.* Greenwillow, 1984.

Silverstein, Shel. *A Light in the Attic.* Harper & Row, 1981.

Silverstein, Shel. *Where the Sidewalk Ends.* Harper & Row, 1974.

Writing Lyric Poetry

Throughout this sourcebook, your students have had many opportunities to try their hand at writing lyric poetry. In addition, they now have their portfolios containing finished poems, rough drafts, and ideas for additional poems.

This section is designed to help students organize and refine their poems and ideas to ready some of their work for a classroom anthology.

Page 42: Reviewing Your Own Poems And Poetry Ideas

With the class, read the directions for activities **1, 2,** and **3**. Provide time periods over the course of two or three days for students to carry them out. You may wish to schedule writing conferences with each student to help them decide which poems in their portfolio they're satisfied with, which they wish to change, and which they want to develop more fully. Then ask students to fill out the chart in **4**. Have them set aside this page to use in the writing conference with their writing partner.

Page 43: Using A Writing Conference To Clear Up Problems

Your writing conference with individual students (see page 42) can help them state their problems cogently on the chart. If students wish, help them review the problems they've stated and discuss their goals for each poem. After students complete the chart, have them set it aside and turn to reading their partner's poems.

Page 44: Using A Writing Conference To Point Out Great Stuff

Have partners take turns reading aloud two of the poems their classmate has presented for the conference. Each partner should fill out the chart on this page as he or she analyzes the poems.

This completed page, too, will serve in the writing conference.

Page 45: Using A Writing Conference To Help You Revise

Ask student partners to assemble their three writing-conference worksheets: their own pages 42, 43, and the page 44 their partner has filled out. Allow a class period for each student to study and discuss the pages with her or his partner.

Page 46: Revise And Publish

The emphasis in **1.** is on deleting and adding, and on correct spelling and legibility. In revising poems, punctuation is usually up to the poet: lines can run on without punctuation, or commas and periods can denote any places where the writer wants the reader to pause or come to a full stop. Though capitalization usually comes after full stops (periods), you might wisely avoid pushing this issue with poetry, except in obvious cases like proper nouns. All in all, you'll get more "real" poetry if you don't hold your students to hide-bound rules about grammar and punctuation when they're writing poems. Use the publishing suggestions on this page in conjunction with any ideas that appeal to you on pages 6 and 7.

WRITING LYRIC POETRY

Reviewing Your Own Poems And Poetry Ideas

1. Go through your portfolio and arrange your writing into the following groups:
   - **A.** Poems I've written and like just as they are
   - **B.** Poems I've written and like but would like to change here and there
   - **C.** Lines and ideas that are the seeds and beginnings of poems I'd like to finish now
   - **D.** Lines, ideas, and poems that don't satisfy me yet and that I'd like to save and work on at another time
2. Soon you'll be asking a writing partner to read at least three of your poems... and even more, if you like! From groups A, B, and C above, choose the poems you'll discuss with your partner.
3. Make the changes you want to make in your poems from Group 2. Build lines and ideas from Group C into poems you like.
4. In the chart below, write the titles of the poems you'll present and the reasons why you like these poems.

TITLE OF MY POEM	WHY I LIKE THIS POEM

Name (s) _____

WRITING LYRIC POETRY

Using a Writing Conference To Clear Up Problems

Prepare for your writing conference by filling in the chart below.

Write the titles of your poems in the column on the left. In the other column, write problems you have about your poems that you'd like your conference partner to help you solve. Examples are given to help you get started.

POEM TITLES	MY PROBLEMS WITH THIS POEM:
EXAMPLE: "A Narrow Path"	**A.** I want to make this poem rhyme, but the rhymes don't seem to come out right. **B.** I compare a narrow path to a snake, but I'm not sure the comparison fits my idea.

* Don't share this page with your writing partner yet! Instead, exchange poems with your partner. Then read your partner's poems and fill out the chart on the next page.

Name (s) _____

Using A Writing Conference To Point Out Great Stuff!

As you study the poems your partner has written, use these two steps:

1. Use the guidelines on page 10 to study your partner's poems. That is, *read aloud, ask and answer questions,* then *read the poem again.*

2. Fill in the chart below for two poems your partner has written. If the poet uses one of the strategies at the left, circle it and give an example under the poem title.

	POEM #1: Title:_____	POEM # 2: Title:_____
SOUND • rhyme		
• alliteration		
• repetition		
FORM OF THE LINES • musical rhythm		
• natural speech patterns		
• lines arranged in a new way		
COMPARING • metaphor		
• simile		
• personification		

Name (s) _____

Using A Writing Conference To Help You Revise

With your writing partner, use pages 42, 43, and 44 to help you decide these things:

1. Discuss page 44: Which of your poems does your writing partner like best?_____

_____

_____

_____

Why does your partner like these poems? _____

_____

_____

_____

2. Discuss page 43: What problems did your partner help you solve with your poems?_____

_____

_____

_____

3. Think about what you wrote on page 42:

   A. Which poems will you revise as a result of your conference? Explain._____

   _____

   _____

   _____

   B. Which poems won't your revise? Explain. _____

   _____

   _____

Name (s) _____

WRITING LYRIC POETRY

Revise And Publish

1. Revise your poems in these ways:

  A. Using your writing partner's suggestions, insert (put in) or delete (take out) words, phrases, or lines that you think will improve your poems.

      delete~~z~~ a character   Take this out

      inser^t a character   Put this in

  B. Check and correct your spelling with a writing partner.

  C. Make final, neat, correct drafts of your poems.

2. Here are some ways you can publish your poems:

  A. Get together with some classmates and organize your poems for a classroom anthology. Anthologies have sections, like Nature, People, and Thoughts and Feelings. But maybe you'll come up with other classifications, like City, Suburbs, and Country; or Past, Present, and Future; or Love, Friendship, and Enemies.

  B. Sometimes poems go together with pictures. Make a visual display of your poems along with photos, news clips, or drawings that match the feelings and ideas.

  C. Poetry is meant to be heard! Plan and present a read-aloud session of Best Poems We've Written. Find tapes of music that goes with your poems and play the music in the background as you read aloud. If you can memorize your poems by heart, this will be even more impressive!

  D. Decide on poems that little kids will like, and present a read-aloud session for younger children in earlier grades in your school.

46 LITERATURE & WRITING WORKSHOP SOURCEBOOK: **LYRIC POETRY**

Name (s) _____

LYRIC POETRY

End Of Unit: Student's Self-Evaluation

Make a mark on the line to chart your response:
I enjoyed working in this unit

0_____**5**_____**10**
not at all   **somewhat**   **a great deal**

My work on this unit was

0_____**5**_____**10**
not as good as my usual   **about average for me**   **my best ever**

In working on this unit, I most enjoyed:

_____ **working on my own.**   _____ **working with a partner.**   _____ **working in a group.**

The poem I most enjoyed reading was _____

because _____

_____

The best thing about working on this unit was _____

_____

The thing I liked least about working on this unit was _____

_____

What I would like to do better as a reader is _____

_____

Something I learned from reading lyric poetry was _____

_____

Something I learned from writing lyric poetry was _____

_____

One way I can improve my writing is _____

_____

LITERATURE & WRITING WORKSHOP SOURCEBOOK: **LYRIC POETRY** **47**

End of Unit: Teacher's Checklist

Student: _____

Reading Comprehension	Mastery					Unsatisfactory
identifies main ideas	5	4	3	2	1	0
recalls details	5	4	3	2	1	0
makes inferences	5	4	3	2	1	0
recognizes the difference between prose and poetry	5	4	3	2	1	0

The Writing Process	Mastery					Unsatisfactory
self-selects topics	5	4	3	2	1	0
researches information	5	4	3	2	1	0
understands chronological order	5	4	3	2	1	0
revises writing	5	4	3	2	1	0
follows ideas to completion	5	4	3	2	1	0
shares writing	5	4	3	2	1	0

Mechanics	Mastery					Unsatisfactory
uses punctuation appropriate to the poem	5	4	3	2	1	0
uses correct grammar	5	4	3	2	1	0